Washington Bucket List Adventure Guide & Journal

Explore 50 Natural Wonders You Must See & Log Your Experience!

Bridge Press

Bridge Press
dp@purplelink.org

Please consider writing a review!
Just visit: purplelink.org/review

ISBN: 978-1-955149-14-3

FREE BONUS

Find Out 31 Incredible Places You Can Visit Next! Just Go To:

purplelink.org/travel

Table of Contents

How to Use This Book

Welcome to your very own adventure guide to exploring the natural wonders of the state of Washington. Not only does this book lay out the most wonderful places to visit and sights to see in the vast state, but it also serves as a journal so you can record your experience.

Adventure Guide
Sorted by region, this guide offers fifty amazing wonders of nature found in Washington for you to go see and explore. These can be visited in any order, and this book will help keep track of where you've been and where to look forward to going next.

Each portion describes the area or place, what to look for, how to get there, and what you may need to bring along. A map is also included so you can map out your destinations.

Journal Your Experience
Following each location description is a blank journal page for you. During or after your visit, you can jot down significant sights encountered, events confronted, people involved, and memories you gained while on your adventure in the journal portion. This will add even more value to your experience and keep a record of your time spent witnessing the greatest wonders of Washington.

GPS Coordinates and Codes
As you can imagine, not all of the locations in this book have a physical address. Fortunately, some of our listed wonders are either located within a national park or reserve or are near a city, town, or place of business. For those who are not associated with a specific location, it is easiest to map it using GPS coordinates.

Luckily, Google has a system of codes that converts the coordinates into pin-drop locations that Google Maps is able to interpret and navigate.

Each adventure in this guide will include both the GPS coordinates along with general directions on how to find the location and Google plus codes whenever possible.

How to find a location using Google Plus:

1. Open Google Maps on your device.
2. In the search bar, type the Google Plus code as it is printed on the page.
3. Once the pin is located, you can tap on "Directions" for step-by-step navigation.

It is important that you are prepared for poor cell signals. It is recommended to route your location and ensure that the directions are accessible offline. Depending on your device and the distance of some locations, you may need to travel with a backup battery source.

About the State

Washington is simply overflowing with natural wonders to visit. The federal government owns more than one-fourth of the state's land, with the National Park Service owning three national parks and five national forests. The Washington State Park System boasts over one hundred state parks. This abundance of well-preserved nature helps to make Washington one of the greatest destinations in the world for hikers, mountain climbers, and all other types of outdoor enthusiasts. You'll find nearly seven hundred miles of hiking trails crisscrossing Washington's state parks alone.

There are five active volcanoes in the state: Mount Baker, Mount Rainier, Glacier Peak, Mount Adams, and Mount St. Helens. Washington is also the most glaciated state in the contiguous United States — just Mount Rainier has roughly twenty five glaciers. Washington is home to nearly *8,000* lakes as well, perfect for fishing, boating, and other water sports.

The Giant Octopus

One of the great legends of Puget Sound is that of King Octopus. Many believe that the biggest octopus in existence lives under the Tacoma Narrows Bridge. For generations, locals have told tales of the 600-pound octopus — some fear that the monster attacks deep-sea divers, while others think the aquatic monarch just wants to be left alone.

There is some truth to this legend. The largest species of octopus in existence is the Giant Pacific Octopus, and this species does live in Puget Sound. However, Giant Pacific Octopuses only live for three-to-five years, and the largest Giant Pacific Octopus on record weighed 156 pounds. They are beautiful creatures, though, and very intelligent. They can also change color and alter their texture to blend in with plants, coral, and rocks.

Fun Fact: Mount Olympus got its name in 1788 when Captain John Meares, a British fur trader, wrote of the peak, "If that not be the home wherein dwell the gods, it is beautiful enough to be, and I, therefore, call it Mount Olympus.'"

Landscape and Climate

Washington has earned its nickname as the "Evergreen State" with its many forests full of spruce, fir, and cedar trees that cover roughly half of the state's land. Located in the Pacific Northwest, the state has a varied and dynamic landscape. The Cascade Mountains are full of lush green hillsides, glistening glaciers, beautiful meadows, scenic lakes, and jewel-blue rivers. Many of the peaks and slopes remain snow-covered all year long. There is also plentiful wildlife. One might find bobcats, cougars, martens, marmots, bears, deer, elk, and even moose in the wilderness of the Cascades.

The land in Western Washington is hilly and mountainous, thanks to the glaciers of the last ice age. That same glacial activity produced the many islands along the Puget Sound. The Olympic Peninsula features rain forests, alpine peaks, legendary waterfalls, and glacier-carved lakes. In the rainforests, you will find giant ferns, blooming orchids, and Sitka spruce trees up to three hundred feet tall.

Eastern Washington is mainly made up of mountains and farmland, but large portions of the landscape give way to strange rock land formations and barren bedrock. This desert was formed by a series of ice age floods and is full of tall, dry waterfalls and deep ravines.

The Cascade Mountains divide Washington into two very different halves. Western Washington is often called the "wet side" of Washington, while Eastern Washington is the "dry side." Western Washington has mild temperatures and is generally wet during all the seasons (though snow is rare) but summer. Meanwhile, the deserts and grasslands of the east are much drier with more dramatically high and low temperatures in the summer and winter, respectively.

Map of Washington

1) North Cascades National Park

North Cascades National Park was founded in 1968 in order to preserve the area's gorgeous mountains, forests, subalpine meadows, plentiful glaciers, and wildlife. The mountains are a great attraction for mountaineers and hikers, and some call them the "American Alps" due to their snow-covered tops. With names like "Mount Despair" and "Desolation Peak," the mountains may seem intimidating, but you'll feel nothing but awe-inspiring joy when you reach their magnificent peaks.

There are countless wonders to experience in North Cascades National Park, but one you should be sure not to miss is Diablo Lake Overlook. Diablo is a man-made reservoir with turquoise waters. The water gets its color from glacier-ground rock silt carried down by streams from the surrounding mountains. You'll be sure to want to snap a few photos, so don't forget your camera!

Best time to visit: Mid-June through late-September.

Required items: No fee is required to enter the park. However, permits are required for all overnight stays in the park's backcountry year-round. For more information about permits for the park, refer to the National Park Service's website. Summer storms are common, so don't forget boots and a raincoat.

Closest city or town: Sedro-Woolley

How to get there: From Sedro-Woolley, head east toward Puget St. for 154 feet. Then turn left at the first cross street onto Puget St. for half a mile. From there, turn right onto WA-20 E/Moore St. and continue to follow WA-20 E for 54 miles until you see the North Cascades Visitor Center on your right.

GPS Coordinates: 48.5384° N, 121.4481° W

Did you know? Humans continually lived in the North Cascades National Park region for as long as 10,000 years.

Journal:

Date(s) Visited:

Weather conditions:

Who you were with:

Nature observations:

Special memories:

2) Mt. Baker-Snoqualmie National Forest

The Mt. Baker-Snoqualmie National Forest is one of the most popular forests to visit in the U.S. It's situated on the west side of the Cascades between the Canadian border and Mt. Rainier National Park. The forest is full of ancient trees, glacier-covered peaks, and beautiful mountain meadows. Mountains are 5,000-to-6,000 feet tall on the south side of the forest, while in the north, they rise up to 7,000-to-8,000 feet. The forest is also home to Mt. Baker, a towering volcano.

Whether you're a veteran of the outdoors or a new hiker, you will find a great adventure here. The forest offers a little bit of everything — bird watching, river rafting, fishing, skiing, snowshoeing, and more.

Best time to visit: With lovely hikes in the spring, summer, and fall and skiing and snowshoeing in the winter, this is a wonderful destination all year long.

Required items: Before you arrive, make sure to check the U.S. Forest Service's website to see whether you need a permit or pass. If you're visiting in the winter, it's important to come equipped with a shovel, tire chains, and a winter weather kit for your vehicle.

Closest city or town: Glacier

How to get there: From Glacier, head south on Bourne St. for 141 feet toward WA-542 W. Then turn left onto WA-542 E and drive for 21.3 miles. Turn right to stay on WA-542 E and take a slight right after 0.7 miles. After 151 feet, turn right, and the Heather Meadows Visitor Center will be on your right.

GPS Coordinates: 47.7659° N, 121.3778° W

Did you know? The Mt. Baker-Snoqualmie National Forest contains more glaciers and snowfields than any of the other national forests in the lower 48 states.

14

Journal:

Date(s) Visited:

Weather conditions:

Who you were with:

Nature observations:

Special memories:

3) Glacier Peak Wilderness

The Glacier Peak Wilderness takes up 566,057 acres of land and features 10,541-foot-tall Glacier Peak, which is the most remote major volcanic peak in the Cascade Range and the fourth-largest peak in the state. Wildlife in this area includes mountain goats, bears, cougars, lynx, martens, wolverines, gray wolves, deer, elk, bear, mountain goat, cougar, marten, and lynx. It's also a great spot for fishing cutthroat trout.

There are as many as one hundred hiking trails ranging from easy to very advanced. The 8.3-mile Green Mountain Trail near Darrington, Washington, features lovely wildflowers. For those less inclined toward hiking, there's horseback riding, bouldering and climbing, and navigating the glaciers. The Ptarmigan Traverse is known as the most beautiful mountaineering route in the country — considering its snowfields, high peaks, crystal clear alpine lakes, and expansive views; it's not hard to see why.

Best time to visit: July to September

Required items: For information on passes and permits, refer to the U.S. Forest Service's website. If you plan to climb, don't forget to pack some glacier glasses to protect your eyes.

Closest city or town: Darrington

How to get there: The North Fork Sauk Trail is one of many ways to enter the wilderness. From Darrington, take the Mountain Loop Hwy. South for sixteen miles to F.R. 49. Turn left and drive 6.4 miles to a fork. Veer left for the Sloan Creek Trail, and it's 0.1 miles to trailhead parking.

GPS Coordinates: 48.0580° N, 121.2882° W

Did you know? Glacier Peak is known for being one of the most explosive volcanoes in Washington. Its last eruption was in 1700.

Journal:

Date(s) Visited:

Weather
conditions:

Who you were with:

Nature observations:

Special memories:

4) Stehekin

Situated at the headwaters of the third deepest lake in America, Lake Chelan, the picturesque Stehekin Valley is surrounded by the peaks of the Cascades. Only about ninety residents live in the valley year-round. This is a great place to enjoy fishing, boating, hiking, skiing, and snowshoeing. It's also wonderful for wildlife viewing — there's a likelihood that you'll spot at least one deer on your hike.

There are guided tours of Stehekin's majestic 312-foot Rainbow Falls and the lower Stehekin Valley. Boat tours of the Stehekin Valley are available as well. You can also take a self-guided tour of the historic Buckner Orchard, the largest Common Delicious apple orchard in North America. If you make your trip during the fall, you can pick and enjoy some ripe apples!

Best time to visit: Late May to October

Required items: For information on camping permits, hiking trails, and fishing regulations, refer to the National Park Service's website. Remember to bring along a light day pack to carry your lunch, camera, etc., on hikes. There is no cell phone reception, so bring a calling card to operate the public phone located near the landing.

Closest city or town: Chelan

How to get there: There are no roads into Stehekin. However, Lake Chelan Boat Company and Stehekin Ferry both provide round-trip ferry rides from Chelan to Stehekin. If you're feeling adventurous, you could also hike or horseback into the Stehekin Valley.

GPS Coordinates: 48.3093° N, 120.6565° W

Did you know? The name "Stehekin" is based on a Native American Salishan word that means "the way through."

Journal:

Date(s) Visited:

Weather conditions:

Who you were with:

Nature observations:

Special memories:

5) Horseshoe Basin

Located in the upper Stehekin River Valley, Horseshoe Basin is a particularly awe-inspiring sight to see. It lies between the Park Creek Pass and the Stehekin River Road. Orange granite spires ring the lip of the basin as glistening waterfalls crash down into the valley. There are wildflowers as far as the eye can see. If you're lucky, you might catch sight of a black bear — just don't get too close!

Hiking in and out of Horseshoe Basin is not for the faint of heart. The trek is between twelve-and-seventeen miles round trip depending on which route you take. and involves a great deal of climbing. Instead of trying to do everything all in one day, you could elect to camp overnight at Pelton Basin.

Best time to visit: July through September

Required items: Refer to the National Park Service's website for information on passes and permits. Water sources are scarce, so be sure to bring plenty of your own. If you plan on doing any backcountry camping, you'll need an airtight food canister to protect yourself and surrounding wildlife.

Closest city or town: Marblemount

How to get there: From Marblemount, bear right on the Cascade River Rd. and cross the Skagit River. Drive ten miles on the paved road, then 13.5 more miles on a dirt road to the Cascade Pass trailhead (3,600 feet).

GPS Coordinates: 48.4857° N, 121.0215° W

Did you know? Horseshoe Basin is home to the Black Warrior Mine, which operated until the mid-1950s and is listed on the National Register of Historic Places.

Journal:

Date(s) Visited:

Weather conditions:

Who you were with:

Nature observations:

Special memories:

6) Baring Mountain

Baring Mountain's imposing north face is one of the most dramatic sights in the Central Cascades. The north face is one of the great sheer mountain walls in the U.S., comparable to those in Yosemite. The mountain is known for a variety of difficult climbing routes that provide spectacular views of the Central Cascades and adjacent valleys. This might not be the best peak for an easy climb, but it sure will give you a great workout!

Less experienced climbers and hikers can enjoy the beauty of Barclay Lake at the base of Baring Mountain. The sight of the mountain's striking northern face from this vantage point simply can't be beaten. You can stroll or sit by the lake and admire the gorgeous view. The Baring Lake hiking trail is a little over two miles, making it perfect for kids.

Best time to visit: April to October is best for hiking and nature trips. The summer months are ideal for climbing.

Required items: A Northwest Forest Pass is required. It is recommended that you bring along an ice axe for more difficult climbs and hikes during the spring and summer.

Closest city or town: Baring

How to get there: From Baring, head northeast on NE 197th Pl. toward 635th Pl. NE, and then turn right at the first cross street onto 635th Pl. NE. From there, continue onto N F 6024/NF-6024 until you reach the Barclay Lake trailhead. Make sure to bear to the left at a fork about 0.2 miles from the highway — the sign can be difficult to see.

GPS Coordinates: 47.7925° N, -121.4593° W

Did you know? Baring Mountain is the third steepest peak in Washington.

Journal:

Date(s) Visited:

Weather conditions:

Who you were with:

Nature observations:

Special memories:

7) Wallace Falls State Park

There's no shortage of forests, lakes, and waterfalls in Washington, but no place manages to showcase these iconic features of the landscape quite like Wallace Falls State Park. With the park's many glorious trails, hikers will swear they've died and gone to heaven. You can hike or snowshoe up the Wallace River to mighty Wallace Falls. Those searching for a longer hike can follow the Greg Ball Trail to Wallace and Jay Lakes.

Other activities to enjoy in the park include rock climbing and swimming. People have spotted several cougars near Wallace Falls and peregrine falcons inhabit the rock cliffs of the Index Town Wall. The park is great for camping and there are also cabins available to reserve that accommodate up to five guests each.

Best time to visit: April until November

Required items: For information on passes and permits, refer to the Washington State Parks' website. The parking lot is large but tends to fill up fast — especially on holidays, weekends from March through October, and in general between 11 a.m. and 3 p.m.

Closest city or town: Gold Bar

How to get there: From Gold Bar, head northwest on Lewis Ave. toward 4th St. for 0.2 miles. Turn right onto 1st St. and drive for 0.3 miles. Take another right onto May Creek Rd. and drive for 1.3 miles until you reach a Y-junction. Go left and drive up a short path to the Wallace Falls State Park parking lot.

GPS Coordinates: 47.8992° N, 121.6718° W

Did you know? The name "Wallace" is derived from the name "Kwayaylsh," the surname of the first homesteaders in the area.

Journal:

Date(s) Visited:

Weather conditions:

Who you were with:

Nature observations:

Special memories:

25

8) Okanogan-Wenatchee National Forest

Okanogan-Wenatchee National Forest is a vast and dynamic landscape, taking up 3.8 million acres along the east slopes of the Cascade Range. The forest is diverse, with tall, glaciated alpine peaks along the Cascade Crest, verdant valleys of ancient trees, and rugged shrub-steppe country at its eastern edge. There are hundreds of miles of hiking trails through the wilderness and options to camp in developed campgrounds or out in the backcountry.

This forest is a paradise when it comes to outdoor recreation — there's something for everyone. You can hunt and fish to your heart's content. Or you can also go horseback riding, rock climbing, mountain biking, drive off-road vehicles, and more. In the winter, there's cross-country and downhill skiing, as well as snowmobiling. There are also Forest Service cabins available for rent.

Best time to visit: Year-round

Required items: Permit requirements vary, so be sure to check the U.S. Forest Service's website. The Washington Department of Fish and Wildlife website provides information on fishing regulations.

Closest city or town: Winthrop

How to get there: The Blue Lake trailhead is one of many ways to access the Okanogan-Wenatchee National Forest. From Winthrop, drive 31.3 miles on WA-20 W until you reach milepost 162. The trailhead is 0.5 miles past milepost 162 on the south side of WA-20 W. There is a paved parking lot with space for twenty cars.

GPS Coordinates: 48.5190° N, 120.6744° W

Did you know? The northern reaches of the Okanogan-Wenatchee are home to one of the largest populations of lynx in the lower 48 states.

Journal:

Date(s) Visited:

Weather
conditions:

Who you were with:

Nature observations:

Special memories:

9) Alpine Lakes Wilderness

The Alpine Lakes Wilderness is one of the most popular locations for outdoor recreation activities in the state. It encompasses roughly 394,000 acres of the Central Cascades region. It has over six hundred miles of hiking trails and is accessible by forty-seven different trailheads.

The wilderness features more than seven hundred lakes and mountain ponds. Several peaks and slopes of the surrounding Cascades are permanently covered in snow. This diverse landscape also includes expansive meadows and dry forestland. In the Enchantment Lakes area, you'll find the Cashmere Crags, which are known for being one of the best rock-climbing sites in the western U.S.

Best time to visit: July through October

Required items: Permit requirements vary, and some trailheads require a recreation pass, so refer to the U.S. Forest Service's website for more information. Proper climbing gear is essential for the Cashmere Crags.

Closest city or town: Leavenworth

How to get there: The Blackpine Trailhead is one of many ways to access the Alpine Lakes Wilderness. From Leavenworth, take US-2 West for 0.8 miles. Turn left onto Icicle Rd. and drive for roughly eighteen miles. The road eventually becomes Forest Rd. 7600 and makes a left turn to cross Icicle Creek. At about the 18-mile point, the Black pine Trailhead will be on your left.

GPS Coordinates: 47.6091° N, 120.9450° W

Did you know? When President Ford signed the law protecting the Alpine Lakes Wilderness Area in 1976, he allegedly said, "anywhere so beautiful should be preserved."

Journal:

Date(s) Visited:

Weather conditions:

Who you were with:

Nature observations:

Special memories:

10) Mount Sawyer

A hike up Mount Sawyer will reward you with vibrant views of wildflower meadows along the way with wild blueberries, huckleberries, and heather surrounding most of the trail. From the top, you can see three hundred and sixty degrees of Cascade Mountains with Glacier Peak and Mount Baker in the north, Mount Baring to the west, and Mount Rainier to the south.

Once you've taken in the view, you can head down the main trail to Sawyer Pass. There you can have lunch amid the heather and huckleberries. Be sure to wear bright colors and make some noise during your visit, as bears and cougars are known to inhabit the area.

Best time to visit: Any time of year — winter for snowshoeing, spring for wildflowers, summer for berry picking, and autumn for colors.

Required items: Refer to the U.S. Forest Service's website for information on passes and permits. Bugs love the wildflowers as much as we do, so remember to pack bug spray!

Closest city or town: Skykomish

How to get there: From Skykomish, head west on E Railroad Ave. toward 5th St N. Then turn right onto 5th St N and take another right onto US-2 E. Look for Foss River Rd. F.S. 68 and take a right. After 2.3 miles, continue onto NF-68. After 1.2 miles, turn left onto NF-6830. Keep right for about a mile, then take a slight right, and in half a mile, you'll reach the Tonga Ridge Trailhead parking lot.

GPS Coordinates: 47.6787° N, 121.2648° W

Did you know? Mount Sawyer was named after George Sawyer, a Skykomish District Ranger who spent his life keeping watch for forest fires until his death in 1930.

Journal:

Date(s) Visited:

Weather conditions:

Who you were with:

Nature observations:

Special memories:

11) Granite Mountain

There are a few different peaks called "Granite Mountain" in the state, but this tall one alongside I-90 has proven the most popular. Granite Mountain is another hike that is not going to be a walk in the park — you need to be in good shape for this one. The hike itself is only 8.6 miles round trip, but you'll have to climb 3,800 feet to a lookout with an elevation of 5,629 feet.

But the views of the Central Cascades are well worth the effort. On this hike, you'll be able to see every volcano in the state, with the exception of Mount St. Helens. The route features high alpine meadows, towering hemlocks, and a historic lookout tower at the summit. Huckleberry bushes line the trail and in late summer can provide a tasty snack. Keep an eye out for pika on your way, which is common in the area.

Best time to visit: Summer for wildflowers and fall for color

Required items: A Northwest Forest Pass is required. If you choose to visit during the winter, take caution due to persistent avalanche hazards, and remember to bring proper gear for a winter outing.

Closest city or town: North Bend

How to get there: From North Bend, head east on I-90 and drive for 16.6 miles. Take Exit 47 and turn left onto Forest Rd. 55. Turn left on Forest Rd. 9034 and continue to the Pratt Lake-Granite Mountain trailhead on your right. From there, hike the Pratt Lake Trail #1007 for one mile, where the junction for Granite Mountain turns sharply to the right and up the hill.

GPS Coordinates: 47.3979° N, 121.4866° W

Did you know? A 1916 mountaineer's journal describes a summer forest lookout station at the summit of Granite Mountain.

Journal:

Date(s) Visited:

Weather conditions:

Who you were with:

Nature observations:

Special memories:

12) Olallie State Park

More than anything else, Olallie State Park is known for its awe-inspiring waterfalls. Hiking trails lead to the mighty Twin Falls, as well as the smaller Weeks Falls and many other waterfalls. Ambitious mountain bikers can attempt the 20-mile Olallie Trail, which provides gorgeous views of the rushing river, lush forests, and unique rock formations of the Snoqualmie Valley.

There are also numerous cliffs for mountain climbing enthusiasts to enjoy. There is excellent fishing on the South Fork of the Snoqualmie River as well. And when you need a break, you can have some lunch at the South Fork Picnic Area.

Best time to visit: Year-round. The river is seasonally open for fishing.

Required items: Olallie State Park has an automated pay station where you can buy a one-day ($10) or annual ($30) Discover Pass. For more information on passes and permits, refer to the Washington State Parks' website. If you plan to rock-climb, proper equipment is mandatory.

Closest city or town: North Bend

How to get there: The Twin Falls trailhead is one of many you can use to access the park. From North Bend, head southwest on N Bend Blvd. N/Bendigo Blvd. N toward W North Bend Way. Then turn left at the first cross street onto N Bend Way/W North Bend Way. Once you reach the traffic circle, go straight onto E North Bend Way. After 3.4 miles, turn left onto 468th Ave. S.E. After that, turn left onto S.E. 159th St. and continue another 0.5 miles to the Twin Falls parking lot.

GPS Coordinates: 47.4530° N, 121.7054° W

Did you know? In 1977, the park's name was changed from Twin Falls State Park to Olallie, the Chinook Jargon word for "salmonberry," due to their berries' abundance in the area.

Journal:

Date(s) Visited:

Weather conditions:

Who you were with:

Nature observations:

Special memories:

13) Rattlesnake Mountain Scenic Area

The Rattlesnake Mountain Scenic Area covers 1,851 acres of the southern mountainous ridge of the Snoqualmie Valley. Here you can find Douglas fir forests, pockets of old-growth forests, cliffs, and steep slopes. Their area is also home to a wide array of wildlife, including northern spotted owls, peregrine falcons, blacktail deer, Roosevelt elk, black bears, cougars, bobcats, coyotes, foxes, and ospreys.

This lovely part of the state offers some of the most scenic hiking in the Cascade foothills. The ridge's 10-mile trail provides views of Mount Si, the upper Snoqualmie Valley, and the Cascades. At the south end, you'll be rewarded with a fantastic view of the Cedar River Watershed from the 1,000-foot-tall ledges above Rattlesnake Lake.

Best time to visit: Year-round, though trails are sometimes snowy in winter

Required items: Refer to the Washington State Department of Natural Resources' website for information on passes and permits.

Closest city or town: North Bend

How to get there: From North Bend, head southwest on N Bend Blvd. N/Bendigo Blvd. N toward W North Bend Way. When you reach the traffic circle, take the second exit onto the I-90 E ramp to Spokane. Merge onto I-90 E and after 1.7 miles, take Exit 32 for 436th Ave. S.E. Turn right onto 436th Avenue, then continue about four miles down the road to the Rattlesnake Lake parking lot on the right.

GPS Coordinates: 47.4308° N, 121.7751° W

Did you know? Rattlesnake Lake received its name around 1850 from Seattle pioneer Arthur A. Denny. The sound of the wind rattling camas seed pods was mistaken as a rattlesnake rattly by a scared road surveyor from Denny's group. Little did he know, there are no poisonous snakes in Western Washington.

Journal:

Date(s) Visited:

Weather
conditions:

Who you were with:

Nature observations:

Special memories:

14) Kendall Katwalk

The name "Kendall Katwalk" may make you a little nervous. Perhaps you're picturing a narrow path on a steep cliff face — and that is definitely one aspect of it. But here, you will also see an old-growth forest, exquisite wildflowers, and spectacular views of the Alpine Lakes Wilderness from both sides of the pass below Kendall Peak.

In late August and early September, you might get the chance to pick some fresh blueberries growing along the trail. Slopes that feature penstemon, lupine, columbine, paintbrush, and phlox are known as Kendall Gardens. Lingering snow can make this gorgeous and dangerous to traverse, though, so be sure to check trail conditions before you arrive.

Best time to visit: June until September

Required items: A Northwest Forest Pass is required. In the winter, you may want to bring snowshoes.

Closest city or town: North Bend

How to get there: From North Bend, drive down N Bend Blvd. N/Bendigo Blvd. N toward W North Bend Way for 0.7 miles. When you reach the traffic circle, take the second exit onto the I-90 E ramp to Spokane. Merge onto I-90 E and, after twenty-one miles, take Exit 52 toward W Summit. Turn left under the freeway onto Alpental Rd., and in 0.1 miles, take the first right. In another 0.1 miles, take a right into the main parking lot.

GPS Coordinates: 47.4522° N, 121.3787° W

Did you know? The Kendall Katwalk was created many years ago by using dynamite to blast a path from Kendall Ridge's sheer granite wall.

Journal:

Date(s) Visited:

Weather
conditions:

Who you were with:

Nature observations:

Special memories:

15) Scenic Hot Springs

Like many of the other most beautiful spots in Washington, Scenic Hot Springs is not for the faint of heart. To reach the pools, you have to hike up into the dense forest, and the trail is at an incline the entire way. But the chance to relax in a hot spring tub in the midst of a gorgeous forest and mountains is well worth the trouble.

After your uphill trek, you will be greeted by the sight of the Scenic Hot Springs. In the fresh air, amongst the trees of the forest, you can enjoy a hot soak in tubs full of natural, crystal clear mineral water. The unpleasant sulfur smell you may associate with hot springs is also completely absent here. Scenic Hot Springs has three hot spring tubs, and each tub fits three to four people. Clothing is optional, so keep that in mind before you visit.

Best time to visit: Year-round

Required items: You are only allowed to visit by invitation, and just ten guests are allowed per day, so make your reservations on the Scenic Hot Springs' website well in advance. You will definitely need some hiking boots to traverse the steep incline. If you're visiting in winter, be sure to bring snowshoes.

Closest city or town: Skykomish

How to get there: From Skykomish, head west on E Railroad Ave. toward 5th St. N, then turn right onto 5th St. N. After 0.2 miles, turn right onto US-2 E and drive for 10.6 miles. The forest road where you need to park is unmarked and comes up pretty suddenly off US-2 E, but when you reserve a spot, you will be emailed detailed directions.

GPS Coordinates: 47.7075° N, 121.1374° W

Did you know? Scenic Hot Springs was originally called Madison Hot Springs and was built in the 1890s to accommodate those who took the train from Seattle to visit the mineral baths.

Journal:

Date(s) Visited:

Weather
conditions:

Who you were with:

Nature observations:

Special memories:

16) Cleman Mountain

Impressively large Cleman Mountain can be seen from pretty much anywhere in the Yakima or Naches Valleys. As the tallest thing in the area, the mountain's summit affords incredible panoramic views of Mount Adams, the William O. Douglas Area, and the Goat Rocks. In the winter, goats, elk, and other animals are easily found wandering the area.

Hiking here, you'll see lovely views over the orchards of Naches Heights and the Naches Valley and down into Waterworks and Meystre Canyons. The climb can range from fairly easy to very difficult depending on the weather and how far you plan to go. A jaunt through the canyon is simple, while reaching the summit requires a great deal of stamina and physical fitness.

Best time to visit: May for wildflowers, September and October for color and wildlife

Required items: Visit the Washington Department of Fish and Wildlife's website for information on passes and permits. While hiking, it's a good idea to carry a backpack with a hip belt to take the pressure off your shoulders.

Closest city or town: Naches

How to get there: From Naches, take US-12 W for 16.9 miles to a junction with Old Naches Rd. on the right. Continue straight past this junction for 0.4 miles on WA-410 W and take an immediate right into the parking area after you cross a small bridge. If you hit the double lane section of WA-410 W, you have gone too far and will need to turn around.

GPS Coordinates: 46.7487° N, 120.7970° W

Did you know? Originally the Cleman Mountain Lookout was developed in 1946 with a log cabin.

Journal:

Date(s) Visited:

Weather
conditions:

Who you were with:

Nature observations:

Special memories:

17) Cowiche Canyon

At just three miles, the Cowiche Canyon trail is one of the shorter ones included in this guide. But there is a lot of beauty and wonder packed into this small package. You'll walk beneath spectacular andesite and basalt cliffs. The trail will also have you crossing Cowiche Creek several times along the way.

If you make your visit in the spring, gorgeous wildflowers will cover the hillsides. The beautiful chirps of songbirds will follow you through the whole hike as well. You may also be lucky enough to catch sight of a lucia azure butterfly or a yellow-bellied marmot.

On the hike, there's a junction with the Winery Trail, which will take you to the Wilridge Vineyard and the Tasting Room of Yakima. If you like, you can take a little side trip to get some delicious wine with glorious views of Mount Adams.

Best time to visit: Spring for wildflowers, fall for color

Required items: The trail is mostly unshaded, so don't forget plenty of water and sunscreen! The "Living with Wildlife" section of the Washington Department of Fish and Wildlife's website provides helpful tips about what to do when you encounter wild animals.

Closest city or town: Weikel

How to get there: From Weikel, head south on Weikel Rd. After twenty-three feet, turn left at the sign for Cowiche Canyon. In 0.3 miles, you'll reach the western Cowiche Canyon trailhead.

GPS Coordinates: 46.6306 ° N, 120.6633° W

Did you know? A railroad through the canyon was completed in 1923 and ran until 1984, when the line was abandoned. Alongside the trail, you can occasionally come across ties from the original railroad and even the remains of the old wagon trail that came before the rail line.

Journal:

Date(s) Visited:

Weather
conditions:

Who you were with:

Nature observations:

Special memories:

18) Sun Lakes-Dry Falls State Park

The Dry Falls surrounding Sun Lakes-Dry Falls State Park is one of the most extraordinary and visually striking geological wonders in the U.S. The former waterfall was created by Ice Age floods over 13,000 years ago and stood four times larger than Niagara Falls. Now, the stark cliff is four hundred feet tall and 3.5 miles wide. It overlooks a desert oasis full of reflective lakes and deep gorges. The historic Vista House Overlook offers panoramic views of Dry Falls.

The park is also a wonderful spot for outdoor recreation. Park Lake is great for boating and swimming, and Deep Lake is a perfect location for deep-paddling and kayaking. Anglers love to visit Dry Falls Lake in search of trout. Plentiful hiking trails wind through the hills and cliffs with incredible views along the way.

Best time to visit: April through September

Required items: Refer to the Washington State Parks' website for information on passes and permits. For fishing regulations and licensing information, visit the Washington Department of Fish and Wildlife's website.

Closest city or town: Coulee City

How to get there: From Coulee City, head west on W Main St. toward N 4th St. Turn right at the 1st cross street onto N 4th St., then turn left onto US-2 W. After 2 miles, turn left onto WA-17 S. Dr. for 2.1 miles then turn left. After 187 feet, take a right, and in fifty-six feet, you'll reach the Dry Falls Visitor Center.

GPS Coordinates: 47.6065° N, 119.3647° W

Did you know? The flow of the floodwater that created Dry Falls was estimated to be ten times more powerful than the combined flow of every river on Earth.

Journal:

Date(s) Visited:

Weather conditions:

Who you were with:

Nature observations:

Special memories:

19) White Bluffs

White Bluffs is a particularly striking part of the state that will give you a change of pace from the forests of the west. Also known as Hanford Reach, White Bluffs is full of sand dunes and high desert with views of the Columbia River. On the other side of the river, you can see the Hanford Campus, where there are reactors that date back to World War II. The rushing rivers and sands that surround you with the expansive sky above will make you feel truly at one with nature.

The area is also rich in wildlife. In the sand, you can find small mammals and lizards, while in the marshier areas, you might catch sight of ravens, ospreys, herons, red-winged blackbirds, and golden and bald eagles. While the White Bluffs South Slope Trail is rated as difficult, the White Bluffs North Slope Trail is appropriate for hikers at all levels of experience, and so, it's perfect for families.

Best time to visit: April through June and September

Required items: There's no shade, so don't forget water, sunscreen, and a hat. If you plan on hiking through the sagebrush, you'll need pants as well.

Closest city or town: Othello

How to get there: From Othello, head south toward S Broadway Ave. for 184 feet. Turn left onto S Broadway Ave. and after two miles, continue onto WA-24 W. Dr. for 15.3 miles, then turn left. After four miles, turn right, and the unsigned north trailhead will be on your right. Near the boat launch, you'll find a small parking area.

GPS Coordinates: 46.6772° N, 119.4446° W

Did you know? Hundreds of years ago, Native American tribes used the White Bluffs area to cross the river and as a place to gather for celebrations and trading.

Journal:

Date(s) Visited:

Weather
conditions:

Who you were with:

Nature observations:

Special memories:

20) Steamboat Rock State Park

Steamboat Rock State Park stretches across 3,522 acres. The land was carved at least 13,000 years ago by Ice Age floods into a breathtaking canyon that features several lakes. The hike to the top of Steamboat Rock offers stunning views of Grand Coulee and the majestic mountains of the Okanogan-Wenatchee National Forest with the blue lake below. At an 800-foot elevation and with a surface area of six hundred acres, Steamboat Rock offers many wonders to behold for avid hikers.

The park is also a great place for water sports, with seven watercraft launches and 320 feet of dock on Banks Lake. Northrup Canyon offers plenty of fun for mountain biking and horseback riding enthusiasts. This place is a well-loved camping park with three campground areas that are protected from strong winds by towering poplar trees. There are three cabins available for rent in the Bay Loop as well that can accommodate up to five guests.

Best time to visit: Year-round

Required items: For information on passes and permits, refer to the Washington State Parks' website. Mosquitoes are common in the summer, so be sure to pack bug spray.

Closest city or town: Grand Coulee

How to get there: From Grand Coulee, head southwest on WA-155 S/Grand Coulee Ave. toward Spokane Blvd. NE, continue to follow WA-155 S for 10.1 miles, and then turn right onto Steamboat Rock Park Entrance Rd. After 2.9 miles, you'll reach the Steamboat Rock Trailhead.

GPS Coordinates: 47.8635° N, 119.1227° W

Did you know? There is a Native American legend that Steamboat Rock was created when Eagle refused to let Coyote marry his daughter.

Journal:

Date(s) Visited:

Weather
conditions:

Who you were with:

Nature observations:

Special memories:

21) Snake River

Snake River is the Columbia River's largest tributary, originating in Yellowstone National Park. The river is home to the Pacific Northwest's biggest whitewater rapids and is a popular spot for river rafting. Snake River flows through Hells Canyon, which is situated along the border of Oregon, Washington, and Idaho. The mighty canyon is deeper than even the Grand Canyon. At Hells Canyon, there are many opportunities for water sports like jet boating and fishing, as well as hiking, hunting, and camping.

If you're in the mood for a gentle stroll along the river, the paved Greenbelt Walkway Trail is ideal. The trail begins at Granite Lake Park then follows the Snake River for almost seven miles to Chief Looking Glass Park in Asotin.

Best time to visit: The summer months are the best time for white water rafting.

Required items: If you plan to go rafting or boating, it's important to bring personal flotational devices suitable for whitewater. For more information on boating permits, visit Recreation.gov.

Closest city or town: Clarkston

How to get there: The Greenbelt Walkway Trail is one of many spots you may choose to visit along the Snake River. From Clarkston, head southwest on Diagonal St toward 6th St. Turn left onto 6th St. and after 0.4 miles, take another left onto Chestnut St. Dr. for 0.3 miles, then turn left onto Beachview Blvd. The Greenbelt Walkway Trail will be on your right.

GPS Coordinates: 46.3823° N, 117.0484° W

Did you know? In 1805, Lewis and Clark famously traveled down the Snake River and reached the Columbia River on October 16. They initially called Snake River "Lewis's River" after Captain Lewis.

Journal:

Date(s) Visited:

Weather conditions:

Who you were with:

Nature observations:

Special memories:

22) Lake Sammamish State Park

Lake Sammamish State Park takes up 531 acres and has 6,858 feet of waterfront on Lake Sammamish. With two lakefront beaches (Tibbetts Beach and Sunset Beach), the park is a fantastic spot for a beach day. It's a popular place for boating, waterskiing, and other watersports. The park includes a boat launch where visitors can park their vehicles and boat trailers.

This park is yet another wonderful hiking location with its many trails through wetlands and deciduous forests. Bald eagles and blue herons nest in the park, so keep an eye out! For more wildlife viewing opportunities, there's also a great-blue-heron rookery and a salmon-bearing creek. There is a state-of-the-art playground for children and picnic areas for the whole family.

Best time to visit: Summer is ideal for swimming and kayaking.

Required items: For information on passes and permits, refer to the Washington State Parks' website.

Closest city or town: Issaquah

How to get there: Head east on E Sunset Way toward 3rd Ave. NE for 0.6 miles, then use the left two lanes to turn left to merge onto I-90 W toward Seattle. After 1.9 miles, take Exit 15 toward WA-900 W/Renton and drive for 0.4 miles. Turn right onto 17th Ave. N.W., then in 0.1-mile turn left onto N.W. Sammamish Rd. and the park will be on your right.

GPS Coordinates: 47.5600° N, 122.0555° W

Did you know? Before State Parks bought the land in 1950, this area was farmed for seventy years. And before *that*, the land was inhabited by Native Americans for thousands of years.

Journal:

Date(s) Visited:

Weather
conditions:

Who you were with:

Nature observations:

Special memories:

23) Cattle Point Lighthouse

Cattle Point is the southernmost tip of San Juan Island. It got its name from when cattle first appeared at the point in 1853 after Hudson's Bay Company established a ranch there. The lighthouse overlooks the Strait of Juan de Fuca, where the Haro Straits meet the San Juan Channel and is a part of the San Juan Islands National Monument.

The hike to the lighthouse is short but oh-so-sweet. Hiking around the windswept area, you'll see grassy dunes and plenty of birds. You may even spy on a few golden eagles soaring through the wind in the sky above. Since the lighthouse is on a point, you will get phenomenal views from a few different angles — it's a great place to watch the sun rise or set. Next, the trail takes you down the water, where you can admire the glacier-carved rocky beach.

Best time to visit: Late spring into autumn

Required items: Refer to the Washington State Department of Natural Resources' website for information on passes and permits.

Closest city or town: Friday Harbor

How to get there: From Friday Harbor, head southeast on Second St. S toward Spring St. Turn right onto Spring St., and after 0.3 miles, turn left onto Mullis St. After 0.7 miles. Continue onto Cattle Point Rd. When Cattle Point Rd. makes an abrupt left turn at the 8.1-mile-point, park in the Department of Natural Resources' picnic and interpretive site.

GPS Coordinates: 48.4506° N, 122.9633° W

Did you know? While a navigational lantern has remained at Cattle Point since 1888, the lighthouse wasn't built until 1935.

Journal:

Date(s) Visited:

Weather
conditions:

Who you were with:

Nature observations:

Special memories:

24) Lopez Hill

Lopez Hill covers four hundred acres, with the hill standing at 535 feet tall. The area is a dream come true for nature lovers and hiking enthusiasts. If you're looking for a challenge, a network of hiking trails weave their way through thick growth forests, canyons, moss-covered rocky outcroppings, and prairie land.

In addition to hikers, the trails are open to mountain bikers and equestrians as well (though some trails are only open to horses on a seasonal basis). Lopez Hill is also a popular destination for hunters. There's a wide range of island flora to behold — including lichens, fungi, wildflowers, and more. The summit affords glorious views of the Strait of Juan de Fuca and beyond. You could easily spend more than one day enjoying the natural wonders of Lopez Hill.

Best time to visit: Year-round

Required items: If you are traveling to Lopez Island by ferry, it is highly recommended that you make reservations, especially from May to September. For more information about traveling by ferry, visit the Lopez Island Chamber of Commerce's website.

Closest city or town: Lopez Island

How to get there: From the Lopez School, head east on School Rd. for 1.2 miles. After that, take a right onto Lopez Sound Rd. and continue for 2.4 miles. Turn right onto a gravel entry road, which ends at the parking area.

GPS Coordinates: 48.4816° N, 122.8698° W

Did you know? The Lopez Hill trails are built and maintained entirely by volunteers. The Friends of Lopez Hill is an organization made up of volunteers who are dedicated to preserving Lopez Hill's natural beauty and recreational value.

Journal:

Date(s) Visited:

Weather conditions:

Who you were with:

Nature observations:

Special memories:

25) Deception Pass State Park

Out of all of Washington's state parks, Deception Pass is the most popular. With gorgeous views, shadowy coves, old-growth forests, rugged cliffs, abundant wildlife, and an iconic high bridge, it's not hard to see why.

This park offers something for everyone. Cranberry Lake is a great spot for swimming and fishing, making it perfect for families. There's plenty of Puget Sound beachfront for relaxing and searching for seashells. It's not unusual to spy a family of seals or even a whale. You can also enjoy Rosario Beach's tide pools and boating at Cornet Bay. For hikers, there are several forests and bluffs to traverse. The park is home to Hoypus Forest, one of the state's oldest remaining old-growth forests.

Best time to visit: June through September

Required items: For information on passes and permits, refer to the Washington State Parks' website. If you plan to hike, you can purchase a hiking map at the Park Office on the Whidbey Island side of Deception Pass Bridge.

Closest city or town: Anacortes

How to get there: From Anacortes, head east on 12th St. toward Commercial Ave. Turn right at the first cross street onto Commercial Ave. and drive for 1.3 miles. At the traffic circle, take the second exit onto WA-20 Spur E. After 0.6 miles, take the second exit at the next traffic circle and stay on WA-20 W for 6.4 miles. Turn right onto Deception Pass State Park, and the Deception Pass Registration Entrance Station will come up on your left.

GPS Coordinates: 48.3930° N, 122.64736° W

Did you know? Names like Rosario Beach and Fidalgo Island date back to 1792 when Spanish Captain Salvador Fidalgo explored the area.

Journal:

Date(s) Visited:

Weather conditions:

Who you were with:

Nature observations:

Special memories:

26) Padilla Bay

Padilla Bay is located between the San Juan Islands and the mainland and is an estuary of the Skagit River. Hiking along the bay is perfect for beginners. On your hike, you'll see a piece of history — an old barn that once belonged to a "stump farm," which is the name for cheap land purchased after the logging area was converted to farming in the early 1900s. Great blue herons like to hunt around the barn, so keep an eye out for them.

You also might catch sight of northern harriers along the shoreline and roses growing wild along the ditch. Birdsong will accompany you on your journey. At low tide, the water will recede from the bay, and you can see the mudflats. At a small promontory, there's a chance to take a rest on a bench to admire the views of Lummi Island and Mount Baker. In the winter, you might spy a snowy owl.

Best time to visit: Year-round

Required items: For information on passes and permits, visit the Pacific Northwest Trail Association's website. This bay is great for birdwatching, so don't forget your binoculars!

Closest city or town: Mount Vernon

How to get there: From Mount Vernon, head north on S 1st St. toward Washington St. for 449 feet, and then turn left onto WA-536 W/W Division St. In five miles, continue straight onto WA-20 W. After 1.7 miles, turn right onto Laconner Whitney Rd. In 256 feet, continue onto Whitney Bayview Rd., and in 0.2 miles, continue onto Bayview Edison Rd. Dr. for 0.6 miles, turn left, and in 135 feet, you'll reach the Padilla Bay Trailhead.

GPS Coordinates: 48.4571° N, 122.4661° W

Did you know? Padilla means "bread pan" in Spanish.

Journal:

Date(s) Visited:

Weather
conditions:

Who you were with:

Nature observations:

Special memories:

27) Larrabee State Park

Larrabee State Park was Washington's very first state park. The camping park is known for its picturesque views of the San Juan Islands and Samish Bay. This park has several fantastic recreation options — you can go paddling, diving, and fishing. Freshwater Lost and Fragrance Lakes provide wonderful trout fishing. The park is also a prime location for shellfish harvesting.

There are plenty of scenic spots throughout the park that are perfect for spending time with family or getting lost in solitary thought. Though the shore is the main draw of this park, hikers won't be disappointed. Larrabee State Park features a Douglas fir and salal forest full of hiking and mountain biking trails.

Best time to visit: The park is open year-round, but the shore is best enjoyed during the summer months.

Required items: For information on camping reservations, as well as passes and permits, refer to the Washington State Parks' website.

Closest city or town: Bellingham

How to get there: From Bellingham, head west on W Champion St. toward W Magnolia St. Turn left onto W Magnolia St., then turn right onto N State St. At the traffic circle, take the second exit onto Blvd., and after 0.8 miles, merge onto S State St. Continue until the road becomes WA-11 S/Chuckanut Dr. N. Turn right onto Larrabee State Park after 5.1 miles, and in 0.1 miles, turn right to stay on Larrabee State Park. In 466 feet, you will reach the Larrabee State Park Campground.

GPS Coordinates: 48.6552° N, 122.4914° W

Did you know? The Larrabee family donated twenty acres to the state in 1915 so that the land could be made into a park. The park was named after Charles Xavier Larrabee and opened to the public in 1923.

Journal:

Date(s) Visited:

Weather
conditions:

Who you were with:

Nature observations:

Special memories:

28) Lime Kiln Point State Park

Thanks to the small park's ample population of gray whales, orcas, and porpoises, Lime Kiln Point State Park is also known as Whale Watch Park. Many believe Lime Kiln Point, at the west end of San Juan Island, is one of the greatest whale-watching spots in the entire world. You can watch the whales from a sea cliff, or perhaps from the historic Lime Kiln Lighthouse. Whale-watching boats and guided kayak trips are also available.

If whale watching isn't your thing, there's still lots of fun to experience here. Diving, hiking, and birdwatching are great activities to pursue during your visit. There are twelve picnic sites scattered along the shoreline and near the lighthouse as well.

Best time to visit: May through September for whale watching

Required items: For information on passes and permits, refer to the Washington State Parks' website. Though whales are sometimes very close, other times they are farther out — so remember your binoculars!

Closest city or town: Friday Harbor

How to get there: From Friday Harbor, head southeast on Second St. S toward Spring St. Turn right onto Spring St. and, after 0.9 miles, continue onto San Juan Valley Rd. Turn left onto Douglas Rd. after 0.7 miles and drive for 1.7 miles. Take a right onto Bailer Hill Rd. and after four miles, continue onto West Side Rd. In 1.6 miles, continue straight onto Lighthouse Rd. In twenty-six feet, you will reach the Lime Kiln Point State Park entrance.

GPS Coordinates: 48.5160° N, 123.1510° W

Did you know? The park is named for the lime kilns used in the area as part of a 19th-century lime-producing operation.

Journal:

Date(s) Visited:

Weather conditions:

Who you were with:

Nature observations:

Special memories:

29) Olympic National Park

Olympic National Park spans nearly a million acres and features a uniquely diverse landscape. Here you'll find old-growth rainforests, glaciated mountains, and more than seventy-five miles of Pacific Coast. The list of outdoor recreational activities available in the park is nearly endless — you can explore tidepools, boat, backpack into the wilderness, and more. The area is excellent for fishing salmon, trout, and char.

The park also features a whopping sixteen campgrounds. At night you can gaze up at the spectacular night sky, unmarred by human-made light. Rangers regularly lead interpretive walks and campfire programs, as well as snowshoe walks at Hurricane Ridge in the winter. This park is a hiker's heaven with trails through temperate rainforests, mountains, lowland forests, and along the coast.

Best time to visit: The park is open year-round with many winter activities. However, the rainforests can get up to fifty inches of rain in the winter, so the best time to visit them is spring through fall.

Required items: Refer to the National Park Service's website for information on fees, passes, permits, reservations, and more.

Closest city or town: Port Angeles

How to get there: From Port Angeles, head northwest on E Front St. toward N Laurel St. Turn left onto N Oak St., then another left onto W 1st St. After 0.9 miles, turn right onto S Race St. and drive for 0.6 miles. Turn left onto E 10th St., then right onto S Washington St. Turn right onto E Park Ave., then left onto Mt Angeles Rd. In 0.2 miles, turn right, and the Olympic National Park Visitor Center will be on your left.

GPS Coordinates: 48.0993° N, 123.4257° W

Did you know? The park was originally dubbed the Mount Olympus National Monument by President Theodore Roosevelt in 1909.

Journal:

Date(s) Visited:

Weather
conditions:

Who you were with:

Nature observations:

Special memories:

30) Olympic National Forest

Olympic National Forest stretches out over 600,000 acres and almost surrounds the Olympic Mountain Range and Olympic National Park. The landscape of the forest varies quite a bit, from lush rainforests to tall mountain peaks to the saltwater fjord of Hood Canal.

In this forest, you'll find rushing rivers, abundant wildflowers, and large lowland lakes. From the mountaintops, you can see incredible views of Puget Sound. The area is ideal for hiking, camping, biking, horseback riding, fishing, and picnicking. There are over 250 miles of hiking trails in Olympic National Forest, including eight nature trails with informational signs regarding the forest's history and unique features.

Best time to visit: The forest is open year-round, but the rainforests can get a lot of rain in the winter, so the best time to visit them is spring through fall.

Required items: For information on passes and permits, refer to the U.S. Forest Service's website. The Olympic National Forest offers a free forest-wide recreation guide called the Olympic Outlook at their forest offices, which you can also view online.

Closest city or town: Eldon

How to get there: The Lena Lake/Brothers Trailhead is one of many ways to access the forest. From Eldon, head east on N Eldon Ln. toward US-101 N for 0.2 miles. Then turn left onto US-101 N, drive for 2.1 miles, and take another left onto N Hamma Rd./NF-25. In 7.6 miles, you'll see the Lena Lake/Brothers Trailhead on your right.

GPS Coordinates: 47.5999° N, 123.1508° W

Did you know? Nearly one-third of the Olympic National Forest is old-growth, meaning the trees have grown without help from humans for hundreds of years.

Journal:

Date(s) Visited:

Weather
conditions:

Who you were with:

Nature observations:

Special memories:

31) Dungeness National Wildlife Refuge

With over 250 species of birds residing here, Dungeness National Wildlife Refuge is an absolute paradise for birdwatchers. Dungeness Spit is one of the longest natural sand spits on Earth. Here you'll find a bay, mudflats, and sandy gravel beaches. But this area isn't without the state's signature lush forest trees as well.

This place is a haven of tranquility for wildlife that need protection from pounding waves and fierce winds. Wildlife watching is unsurprisingly a popular activity on the Refuge, as are hiking and photography. The hike to the spit's historic lighthouse is nice and flat, good for less experienced hikers. At the lighthouse, you'll get the chance to have a bite at one of the picnic tables and refill your water before you carry on your scenic journey.

Best time to visit: The best time to see the birds is during their spring and fall migrations.

Required items: Visit U.S. Fish & Wildlife Service website for information on permits, passes, fees, and more.

Closest city or town: Sequim

How to get there: From Sequim, head west on E Washington St. toward S Sequim Ave., turn left at the first cross street onto S Sequim Ave., and drive for 0.4 miles. Then turn right onto US-101 W toward Port Angeles and continue for 4.6 miles. Turn right on Kitchen-Dick Rd., which will become Lotzgesell Rd. Turn left onto Voice of America Rd. W into the Dungeness Recreation Area. Drive through the Recreation Area to the Refuge parking lot.

GPS Coordinates: 48.1412° N, 123.1886° W

Did you know? In 1792, Captain George Vancouver named Dungeness Spit after a famous headland on the south coast of Kent.

Journal:

Date(s) Visited:

Weather
conditions:

Who you were with:

Nature observations:

Special memories:

32) Rialto Beach

At Rialto Beach's rocky shores, you'll find crashing waves, huge drift logs, and magnificent views of offshore islands. A hike here will have you walking over rock, sand, and driftwood. This is a fantastic location for wildlife viewing — there are eagles and seabirds in the sky and otters, sea lions, and whales offshore. There are picnic tables near the parking lot where you can grab a snack or some lunch.

At a rocky arch called Hole-in-the-Wall, you can explore the tidepools and take in the marvelous views. Know that to get to Hole-in-the-Wall; you may need to get your feet wet crossing a creek. Mora Campground is just three miles from the beach and has ninety-four sites. The Mora area is surrounded by lush trees.

Best time to visit: April through October

Required items: Refer to the National Park Service's website for information on permits, reservations, camping, and more. The high tide can make certain parts of the coast impassable, so make sure to always carry a tide table with you. Tide tables are available at coastal ranger stations and visitor centers.

Closest city or town: Forks

How to get there: From Forks, head north on US-101 N/S Forks Ave. toward E Division St. for 1.5 miles. Turn left onto WA-110 W/La Push Rd and drive for 7.8 miles. Then take a right on Mora Rd., drive five miles, and you'll reach the trailhead at the end of the road.

GPS Coordinates: 47.9173° N, 124.6394° W

Did you know? Famed musician Claude Alexander Conlin named the beach after the Rialto theater chain.

Journal:

Date(s) Visited:

Weather conditions:

Who you were with:

Nature observations:

Special memories:

33) Cape Flattery

Cape Flattery has the distinction of being the most northwesterly point in the lower 48 states. It is also the Olympic Coast National Marine Sanctuary's northern boundary. From the tip of the scenic Cape Flattery Trail, you can see a lovely view of Tatoosh Island. You might spy some sea lions on Snake Rock, which lies east of Tatoosh Island. Gray whales are also often sighted off the Cape.

There are four different observation decks on the trail, which provide amazing views of birds, craggy rocks, and gorgeous Pacific waters. Depending on the weather and cloud cover, the Pacific may appear to be a variety of different colors — including shades like light yellow and pink at sunset. You can enjoy a packed lunch or snack at one of the picnic tables at the end of the trail.

Best time to visit: Year-round

Required items: Cape Flattery is managed by the Makah Tribe. Visit their website for information about where to attain recreation permits. There are no trash cans on the trail, so bring something in which to pack any litter.

Closest city or town: Neah Bay

How to get there: From Neah Bay, head northwest on 1st St. toward Fort St. Turn left at the first cross street onto Fort St., then turn right at the second cross street onto 3rd Ave. Turn left onto Cape Flattery Rd., and drive for 3.2 miles. Continue onto Cape Loop, and after 4.4. miles, you'll reach the Cape Flattery parking area.

GPS Coordinates: 48.3831° N, 124.7144° W

Did you know? Named by British explorer James Cook in 1788, Cape Flattery is the oldest permanently named feature in the state.

Journal:

Date(s) Visited:

Weather
conditions:

Who you were with:

Nature observations:

Special memories:

34) La Push Beach

La Push Beach is actually a series of three beaches: First Beach, Second Beach, and Third Beach. The northernmost beach, First Beach, has recreational activities to enjoy all year long. In fall and winter, you can storm watch, then there's hiking in the summer, and you can fish and surf in the spring. It's also the only beach of the three that you can access with a vehicle, while the other two each require a bit of a hike.

Second Beach is the longest, flattest beach of the three. Here. you'll have a great view of sea stacks and surrounding islands. The Quillayute Needles National Wildlife Refuge protects various species of seabirds in the area, making it ideal for birdwatching. There's a 1.5-mile hike from the road to reach Third Beach, the most southern and secluded beach. On the hike through the coastal forest, you'll find terrific views of Strawberry Bay. The beach features sea stacks and driftwood. In the cove at Taylor Point, there is also a picturesque waterfall and tidepools to explore.

Best time to visit: Summer

Required items: For information on passes, camping permits, reservations, and more, refer to the National Park Service's website. La Push is sacred to the Quileute Tribe, so be sure to review the tribe's etiquette requests on the Quileute Nation's website.

Closest city or town: Forks

How to get there: For Third Beach, head north from Forks on US-101 N/S Forks Ave. toward E Division St., and drive for 1.5 miles. Then turn left onto WA-110 W/La Push Rd. After 11.6 miles, the Third Beach Trailhead will be on your left.

GPS Coordinates: 47.8906° N, 124.5992° W

Did you know? The best time for spotting eagles is around 6 p.m. when they dive into the ocean to catch their dinner.

Journal:

Date(s) Visited:

Weather conditions:

Who you were with:

Nature observations:

Special memories:

35) Long Beach

Long Beach got its name from being — not so surprisingly — a very long beach. There's an archway in the town of Long Beach that proclaims the beach to be "The World's Longest Beach," which it is not. But at roughly twenty-eight miles long, Long Beach *is* the world's longest continuous beach on a peninsula. Here, you can sunbathe to your heart's content, enjoy picnics, and go horseback riding. The beach is also a great spot for bird and whale watching, fishing, oystering, and crabbing.

Long Beach is home to the annual Washington State International Kite Festival, where you can watch expert kite fliers fill the sky with vibrant colors. Another thing that makes Long Beach unique is that it's a beach you can drive on. There's nothing quite like driving across the sand with the waves crashing beside you. Just remember to keep to the right and obey the 25-mph speed limit.

Best time to visit: If you want to catch the Washington International Kite Festival, it takes place during the third week of August.

Required items: A four-wheel-drive vehicle isn't essential for driving on the beach, but it is helpful.

Closest city or town: Long Beach

How to get there: The main stretch of beach has seven different access points on the peninsula, which the locals call "beach approaches." For the Seaview Approach, head south on Pacific Ave. toward 2nd St. NE for 1.5 miles from Long Beach. Turn right onto 38th Pl., and in 0.4 miles, the Seaview Beach Approach will be on your right.

GPS Coordinates: 46.3306° N, 124.0635° W

Did you know? More than 150 species of birds live on the peninsula, including the endangered snowy plover and the great horned owl.

Journal:

Date(s) Visited:

Weather conditions:

Who you were with:

Nature observations:

Special memories:

36) Cape Disappointment

Located on the southwesternmost corner of Washington State, Cape Disappointment is a headland where the Pacific Ocean meets the Columbia River. Cape Disappointment State Park and the historic Cape Disappointment Lighthouse are both located on the Cape. The Cape Disappointment Lighthouse was built in 1856 and is the oldest lighthouse in the Pacific Northwest that is still in operation. There is also the operational North Head Lighthouse, which is an easier hike.

The views on the hiking trails of 2,023-acre Cape Disappointment State Park are absolutely awe-inspiring — they will take you around blue lakes, old-growth forest, rugged beaches, and saltwater marshes. Baker Bay is a popular location for boating, while Benson Beach is great for fishing salmon and crab, as well as clam-digging. The park has 137 campsites, and yurts and cabins are also available for rent.

Best time to visit: June through September

Required items: For information on passes, permits, reservations, and more, refer to the Washington State Parks' website.

Closest city or town: Ilwaco

How to get there: From Ilwaco, head south on First Ave. N toward Spruce St. E. At the 1st cross street, turn right onto Spruce St. W. After 328 feet, turn left onto 2nd Ave. S.W. and drive for 0.2 miles. Continue onto WA-100 South/Robert Gray Dr. In 0.8 miles; you'll reach the park entrance at a four-way stop.

GPS Coordinates: 46.2996° N, 124.0654° W

Did you know? Like Mount Olympus, Cape Disappointment was named by British fur trader John Meares in 1788. The sea captain approached the Cape but could not find the river's entrance, much to his "disappointment."

Journal:

Date(s) Visited:

Weather conditions:

Who you were with:

Nature observations:

Special memories:

37) Columbia River Gorge National Scenic Area

The Columbia River Gorge is a vast, 4,000-foot-deep canyon that forms the boundary of Washington to the north and Oregon to the south. Here you can see the Columbia River flow right through the Cascade Mountain Range. The diverse landscape spans between dry grasslands and temperate rainforests. The forests are full of western hemlock, bigleaf maples, and Douglas fir. The deep cut of the gorge is a popular location for kiteboarding and windsurfing thanks to the atmospheric pressure differentials east and west of the Cascades that generate 35-mph winds. This is a great area for biking, hiking, water sports, and salmon-fishing. There's a wealth of amazing panoramic views to be seen along the Pacific Crest Trail. Cape Horn is strenuous but will reward you with sights of wildflowers, waterfalls, and several species of birds.

Best time to visit: Late April through June for wildflowers; July and August for ideal weather

Required items: Both the U.S. Forest Service and Washington State Parks websites provide information on passes, permits, camping reservations, and more.

Closest city or town: Lyle

How to get there: The Balfour-Klickitat Trailhead is one of many ways to access the Columbia River Gorge National Scenic Area. From Lyle, head southwest on 3rd St. toward Klickitat St., turn right at the second cross street onto WA-14 W and drive for 0.3 miles. Turn right onto Canyon Rd./Old Hwy. 8/Old Hwy Number 8. After 0.2 miles, turn right, and in 187 feet, the Balfour-Klickitat Trailhead will be on your left.

GPS Coordinates: 45.6993° N, 121.2935° W

Did you know? Humans have inhabited the Columbia River Gorge for over 13,000 years.

Journal:

Date(s) Visited:

Weather
conditions:

Who you were with:

Nature observations:

Special memories:

38) Mount Rainier

When you think of mountains in Washington, Mount Rainier is likely the first one that comes to mind. At 14,410 feet above sea level, this mighty mountain has definitely earned its fame. The active volcano is the most glaciated peak in the lower 48 states.

Here you'll find vibrant wildflowers around the snow-topped volcano while ancient forests blanket its lower slopes. There are over 260 miles of hiking trails to enjoy at Mount Rainier National Park. These trails will lead you through subalpine meadows, river valleys, and old-growth forests. You'll wander amongst picturesque lakes, rivers, and streams and explore the glaciers.

Best time to visit: July and August for wildflowers. To avoid the crowds, try a spring or fall visit.

Required items: Refer to the National Park Service's website for information on passes, permits, camping reservations, and more. From November 1 through May 1, it is required that all vehicles carry tire chains. If you are planning to ski, snowshoe, or camp in the winter backcountry, be sure to bring a map, compass, and GPS with extra batteries.

Closest city or town: Ashford

How to get there: The Henry M Jackson Visitor Center is one of many ways to access Mount Rainier. From Ashford, head east on WA-706 toward 305th Ave. E for 6.8 miles, then continue onto Paradise Rd. E. After 16.6 miles, turn left. In 144 feet, the Henry M Jackson Visitor Center will be on your left.

GPS Coordinates: 46.7859° N, 121.7368° W

Did you know? The last time Mount Rainier erupted was about 1,000 years ago.

Journal:

Date(s) Visited:

Weather
conditions:

Who you were with:

Nature observations:

Special memories:

39) Nisqually River

The glacial-fed Nisqually River starts on the southern slope of Mount Rainier and flows for seventy-eight miles, eventually terminating in the Puget Sound. Moving down the river, you'll find a scenic landscape of forests, mountains, and rolling farmland.

The beautiful river is a popular destination for fishing enthusiasts. The river's waters are rich with rainbow and cutthroat trout, as well as various species of salmon. Swimming and boating are some other popular activities in the summer. Don't forget to check out the Nisqually River Water Trail, where you can float down the river on non-motorized watercraft and take in the gorgeous views.

There are plenty of opportunities along the river for mountain biking, hiking, and horseback riding. For you, birdwatchers, the area is home to bald eagles, peregrine falcons, marbled murrelets, northern goshawks, pileated woodpeckers, and northern spotted owls.

Best time to visit: October for fishing

Required items: For information on passes and fees, visit the National Park Service's website. Refer to the Washington Department of Fish and Wildlife's website for information on fishing access permits, licenses, and regulations. If you are boating, fishing, or swimming, a lifejacket is essential.

Closest city or town: Ashford

How to get there: This is one of many ways to access the Nisqually River. From Ashford, head east on WA-706 toward 305th Ave. E for 5.6 miles, and the Nisqually entrance to Mt. Rainier National Park.

GPS Coordinates: 46.7408° N, 121.9177° W

Did you know? In the U.S., the Nisqually River is the only river with headwaters in a national park and a delta in a national wildlife refuge.

Journal:

Date(s) Visited:

Weather
conditions:

Who you were with:

Nature observations:

Special memories:

40) Gifford Pinchot National Forest

Gifford Pinchot National Forest is a place the offers a bit of everything. At the Mount St. Helens National Volcanic Monument, there are two hundred hiking trails — some of which are paved and perfect for a beginner, while others are more difficult hikes that will appeal to veteran hiking enthusiasts and backpackers. In the forest's 180,000 acres of wilderness, you can enjoy horseback riding, climbing, fishing, and hunting.

The Cowlitz Valley offers spectacular views of Mount St. Helens to the west, Mount Rainier to the north, and Mount Adams to the east. In the Mount Adams area, you'll find old-growth forests, wetland areas, glistening lakes, glaciers, and scenic meadows. The Mount St. Helens area features spectacular crater views. The area also has opportunities to picnic, hike, and mountain bike at Smith Creek and venture into the Mount Margaret Backcountry.

Best time to visit: Late spring through early fall

Required items: Refer to the U.S. Forest Service's website for information on passes and permits. If you're planning on visiting the backcountry before midsummer, come equipped to cross snow slopes.

Closest city or town: Cougar

How to get there: The Pine Creek Information Center is one of many ways to access the forest. From Cougar, head north toward WA-503 Spur and turn right onto WA-503 Spur. After 3.1 miles, continue onto Rd. 90. In 0.8 miles, Rd. 90 becomes Rd. No 90. In 2.6 miles, continue onto NF-90, and drive for 9.2 miles. NF-90 becomes Hwy. 90, and in 2.5 miles, the Pine Creek Information Center will be on your left.

GPS Coordinates: 46.0626° N, 122.0292° W

Did you know? The Gifford Pinchot National Forest covers 1,368,300 acres, which is bigger than the state of Delaware.

Journal:

Date(s) Visited:

Weather
conditions:

Who you were with:

Nature observations:

Special memories:

41) Indian Heaven

Indian Heaven is a volcanic field surrounded by the 20,784-acre Indian Heaven Wilderness. At 5,927 feet, Lemei Rock is the highest point in the field. Lemei Rock's crater contains the picturesque Lake Wapiki. This area is known for its colorful wildflowers in the summer. The wilderness is a high forested plateau with plentiful meadows and over 150 lakes. The lakes are great for fishing rainbow and brook trout.

With gorgeous colors, lush forests, and plentiful wildlife, this is a wonderful destination for hiking enthusiasts. On a hike, you may catch sight of a deer or elk and get the chance to snack on some ripe huckleberries. The area is also popular with bikers and horseback riders.

Best time to visit: Autumn for the fall colors

Required items: Visit the U.S. Forest Service's website for information on permits and passes. Refer to the Washington Department of Fish and Wildlife's website for fishing license and regulations information. Biting insects tend to swarm in the summertime, so bug spray is a must.

Closest city or town: Trout Lake

How to get there: From Trout Lake, head northwest on WA-141 N toward Jennings Rd. for 5.8 miles. Continue onto Carson Guler Rd./NF-24, and after two miles, turn right onto NF-24/Twin Buttes Rd. Drive for nine miles, and the Cultus Creek Campground will be on your left, where you can find the trailhead for Indian Heaven Trail #33.

GPS Coordinates: 46.0480° N, 121.7546° W

Did you know? The Wasco, Klickitat, Cascades, Umatilla, Yakama, and Wishram tribes gathered in the Indian Heaven area to fish, hunt, and pick berries intermittently over the past 9,000 years.

Journal:

Date(s) Visited:

Weather conditions:

Who you were with:

Nature observations:

Special memories:

42) Goat Rocks Wilderness

The Goat Rocks Wilderness spreads across 108,023 acres between Mount Rainier and Mount Adams and provides beautiful views of Cascade peaks and volcanoes. The Goat Rocks that the wilderness surrounds are the ancient remains left behind from a volcano that existed two million years ago. At 8,201 feet, Gilbert Peak is the highest point in the Goat Rock ranges.

Below the ridges are alpine meadows filled with small glacial lakes and ponds. In this area, you might see marmots, pikas, deer, and elk. The mountain goats for which the area is named are found at high elevations. The wilderness features 120 miles of trails. Many hikers believe that Goat Rocks is the most scenic area along the northern half of the 2,650mile-long Pacific Crest Trail.

Best time to visit: Late July through October

Required items: Visit the U.S. Forest Service's website for information on passes, permits, and camping regulations. Black flies, gnats, and mosquitoes are common in this area, so bring bug spray.

Closest city or town: Packwood

How to get there: The Packwood Lake Trailhead is one of many ways to access the Goat Rocks Wilderness. From Packwood, take US-12 E for 0.3 miles, and turn right onto Snyder Rd. After 1.2 miles, continue onto NF-1260. In 0.4 miles, turn right to stay on NF-1260, and in 3.5 miles, keep left. In another 0.5 miles, you'll reach the Packwood Lake Trailhead.

GPS Coordinates: 46.6085° N, 121.6280° W

Did you know? The Goat Rocks area features four major glaciers: McCall Glacier, Packwood Glacier, Meade Glacier, and Conrad Glacier.

Journal:

Date(s) Visited:

Weather conditions:

Who you were with:

Nature observations:

Special memories:

43) Lewis and Clark Trail State Park

Full of forests of maple, cottonwood, alder, and long-needled ponderosa trees, Lewis and Clark State Park is an oasis of lush greenness in the middle of the arid landscape of Southeastern Washington. In 1806, the Lewis and Clark Corps of Discovery camped out in this area as they made their way home after their journey to the Pacific Coast.

This is a great spot for hiking and camping. With 1,333 feet of freshwater shoreline, Touchet River is also a popular location for wading, tubing, swimming, and fishing for rainbow trout. Birdwatchers can delight in the orange-crowned warblers, red-tailed hawks, and common mergansers that inhabit the area. After a day of fun in the sun, you can visit the local winery half a mile east of the park for a nice glass of wine.

Best time to visit: April through October

Required items: For information on passes, permits, and camping reservations and fees, refer to the Washington State Parks' website. Visit the Washington Department of Fish and Wildlife's website for fishing license and regulations information. The trail gets muddy in the spring, so wear shoes you don't mind getting dirty.

Closest city or town: Dayton

How to get there: From Dayton, take US-12 W/E Main St. for 5.7 miles, and turn right into Lewis and Clark Trail State Park. There's a gravel parking lot near the entrance.

GPS Coordinates: 46.2884° N, 118.0725° W

Did you know? Woolly mammoth fossils — Washington state's official fossil — have been discovered in this area.

Journal:

Date(s) Visited:

Weather
conditions:

Who you were with:

Nature observations:

Special memories:

44) Blue Mountains

The Blue Mountains are often thought to be one of the best-kept hiking secrets in the state. Here, rushing rivers form deep caverns through the peaks. There are hundreds of trails through these picturesque mountains. The best part is that even the most popular trails are less heavily trafficked than those in the Cascades, so you can avoid the crowds and enjoy the tranquility of the nature around you with the big sky above.

The Bluewood Ski Area is a fantastic spot for tree skiing and powder. The area has a large Rocky Mountain elk population, so you may be lucky enough to spot one. Elk hunting is also popular, though it is strictly regulated by the Washington Fish and Wildlife Department.

Best time to visit: Early December to early April for skiing

Required items: For information on Sno-Park permits, visit the Washington State Parks' website. In case of rain, don't forget a waterproof jacket.

Closest city or town: Dayton

How to get there: The Teepee Trailhead is one of many ways to access the Blue Mountains. From Dayton, head west on Patit Rd. and turn left onto E Main St. Take a left onto S 4th St., then make another left onto E Mustard St. and continue onto Eckler Mountain Rd. In 4.1 miles, turn left onto Eckler Mountain Rd/Kendall Skyline Rd., and drive for 22.5 miles. Then turn left onto NF-4608 and continue onto NF-090. In 0.1 miles, you will reach the trailhead.

GPS Coordinates: 46.1182° N, 117.7147° W

Did you know? The range got its name from the beautiful blue color the mountains appear to be from a distance.

Journal:

Date(s) Visited:

Weather conditions:

Who you were with:

Nature observations:

Special memories:

45) Palouse Falls

Palouse Falls State Park is a must-see for fans of Ice Age floods. Palouse Falls was carved over 13,000 years ago and is one of the last active waterfalls on the Ice Age floods path. The waterfall is 198 feet tall and surrounded by basalt cliffs. The place is a paradise for photographers and painters — the glorious falls rushing down in the changing light are a sight that just begs to be documented.

There are three different viewpoints from which you can see the falls. The lowest view is the most direct, while the second features an interpretive path with facts about the canyon. Fryxell Overlook is the highest viewpoint, and from here, you can see marvelous panoramic views of Palouse River Canyon and the falls. The surrounding park is a popular location for picnicking and birdwatching.

Best time to visit: Sunset, year-round

Required items: For information on regulations, passes, and camping fees, refer to the Washington State Parks' website. Take along plenty of water and be aware that there is no phone service at the falls.

Closest city or town: Perry

How to get there: From Perry, head northeast toward WA-261 S for 0.3 miles, turn left onto WA-261 N, and drive for 5.1 miles. Turn right onto Palouse Falls Rd., and in 2.4 miles, you'll reach the Palouse Falls State Park parking area.

GPS Coordinates: 46.6638° N, 118.2273° W

Did you know? Palouse Falls was designated Washington's state waterfall in 2014. The bill advocating for the designation was written by local schoolchildren.

Journal:

Date(s) Visited:

Weather
conditions:

Who you were with:

Nature observations:

Special memories:

46) Columbia Plateau Trail State Park

The 130-mile-long Columbia Plateau State Park Trail is a favorite of hikers and mountain bikers alike. There are thirty-eight miles of hiking trails, another thirty-eight miles of biking trails, and thirty-four miles of horse trails. The park offers views of rolling landscapes and wide-open skies above. Passing the Turnbull National Wildlife Refuge, you'll encounter a whopping two hundred species of birds, as well as elk, moose, deer, and small mammals. On the 23-mile Fish Lake trail, there will be breaks for rest and swimming.

At the southern boundary of the Columbia Plateau Trail, you can hike along the Snake River. There's a lower grade hike that's much easier for beginners, and a higher grade, rockier hike where you'll get to see remnants of an old rail line.

Best time to visit: Year-round

Required items: For information on passes and permits, refer to the Washington State Parks' website.

Closest city or town: Cheney

How to get there: From Cheney, head northeast on 1st St. toward College Ave. for one mile, and then turn right onto Cheney Spokane Rd., and drive for 2.9 miles. Turn right onto S Myers Park Rd., and in 0.2 miles, you'll reach the Fish Lake Trailhead.

GPS Coordinates: 46.3899° N, 118.6807° W

Did you know? The Spokane, Portland, and Seattle Railway Company constructed a rail bed in the Columbia Plateau Trail State Park area in the early 1900s, but the company never actually connected the line from Portland to Seattle. The line was eventually abandoned in 1987 and bought by State Parks in 1991.

Journal:

Date(s) Visited:

Weather
conditions:

Who you were with:

Nature observations:

Special memories:

47) Colville National Forest

Many might think that Washington is entirely flat on the eastern side of the Cascades, but Colville National Forest proves that they are mistaken. This forest was formed by Ice Age glaciers 10,000 years ago and spanned across 1.5 million acres. It features the major valleys of the San Poil-Curlew, Pend Oreille, and Columbia Rivers. Troughs of valleys separate the Kettle River, Selkirk, and Okanogan Mountain Ranges. The forest is full of glistening lakes, rivers, and streams.

With 486 miles of hiking trails, the forest is a wonderful hiking destination. The area is also great for horseback riding, mountain biking, and camping. The forest serves as a habitat for bald eagles, cougars, and grizzly bears. Colville is also home to the last remaining caribou herd in the country.

Best time to visit: Year-round

Required items: For information on passes, permits, and camping reservations, refer to the U.S. Forest Service's website.

Closest city or town: Newport

How to get there: The Upper Wolf Trailhead is one of many ways to access the Colville National Forest. From Newport, head east on 2nd St. and turn left at the 1st cross street onto S Union Ave. After 0.3 miles, turn left onto W Walnut St., and continue onto WA-20 W. Turn left onto Larch S.t, then make a right onto Laurelhurst Dr. In 0.5 miles, the Upper Wolf Trailhead will be on your left.

GPS Coordinates: 48.1903° N,-117.0533° W

Did you know? The Colville Forest Reserve was created by Theodore Roosevelt on March 1, 1907.

Journal:

Date(s) Visited:

Weather conditions:

Who you were with:

Nature observations:

Special memories:

48) Selkirk Range

The Selkirk Mountain Range stretches from Northern Idaho to Eastern Washington to southeastern British Columbia. These mountains are home to the Salmo-Priest Wilderness, where badgers, pine martens, bighorn sheep, mule deer, lynx, black bears, white-tailed deer, elk, moose, cougars, and bobcats reside. Endangered and threatened species like grizzly bears, gray wolves, and the rare woodland caribou also make their home in this wilderness.

Something unique to check out in the Selkirk Mountains is the scenic International Selkirk Loop, a 280-mile road that snakes through breathtaking views of the range. On the road, you will see crystal-clear lakes and rivers amongst the mountains and get many opportunities to hike, fish, and camp. The loop features five hundred miles of trails, many of which lead to waterfalls hidden in the mountains.

Best time to visit: Summer and fall for wildflowers

Required items: For information on passes, permits, and camping reservations, refer to the U.S. Forest Service's website.

Closest city or town: Colville

How to get there: The Abercrombie Trailhead is one of many ways to access the Selkirk range. From Colville, take WA-20 E /E 3rd Ave., and turn left on Aladdin Rd. after 0.9 miles. Drive for 25.5 miles and turn right onto Deep Lake Boundary Rd. Turn right onto Silver Creek Rd., turn left onto NF07078, then take a right onto NF-300. In 3.1 miles, the Abercrombie Trailhead will be on your left.

GPS Coordinates: 48.9322° N, -117.4827° W

Did you know? Some of the rocks found in the Selkirk Mountains are estimated to be about 600 million years old.

Journal:

Date(s) Visited:

Weather conditions:

Who you were with:

Nature observations:

Special memories:

49) Riverside State Park

No matter what type of activities you enjoy, there are plenty of recreational opportunities for you at Riverside State Park. You can go mountain biking, hiking, rock climbing, horseback riding, and more. There are fifty-five miles of hiking and mountain biking trails with various paths to suit every possible level of hiking experience. Hiking around the Bowl and Pitcher area, you'll get beautiful views of the impressive Spokane River, towering Ponderosa firs, and rocky outcroppings.

The park has twenty-five miles of equestrian trails, an obstacle course, and a horse-friendly campground. This is also a good area for boating, fishing, and water sports. In the winter, you can enjoy cross-country skiing, snowshoeing, and snowmobiling. The Bowl and Pitcher Campground features sixteen standard campsites.

Best time to visit: Year-round

Required items: For information on passes, permits, and camping reservations, refer to the Washington State Parks' website.

Closest city or town: Nine Mile Falls

How to get there: The Deep Creek Trailhead is one of many ways to access the park. From Nine Mile Falls, head southeast on W Charles Rd./Rte. 1 toward W Hill Ave. In 0.4 miles, turn right onto WA-291 E/N Nine Mile Rd., and drive for four miles. Turn right onto N Seven Mile Rd., and in 0.6 miles, continue onto W 7 Mile Rd. Drive for 1.5 miles, and turn right onto N State Park Dr. In 0.4 miles, you will reach the trailhead.

GPS Coordinates: 47.7542° N, 117.5488° W

Did you know? Riverside was historically a fur trade hub for Native Americans.

Journal:

Date(s) Visited:

Weather conditions:

Who you were with:

Nature observations:

Special memories:

50) Channeled Scablands

The Channeled Scablands may be in the same state as Western Washington's evergreen forests and snowy-peaked mountains, but it seems like an entirely different world. The scablands are comprised of strange rocky land formations and barren bedrock. The bedrock is crisscrossed by coulees (long channels), which is where the Channeled Scablands got their name.

With its fascinating landscape, this geological wonder is a fantastic area for a scenic drive. There are also several great hikes you can take around the coulees. An easy hike around Twin Lakes will provide gorgeous views of lakes, marshes, and wetlands, as well as vibrant wildflowers and geese, ducks, bald eagles, and ospreys for birdwatchers.

Best time to visit: April through September

Required items: For passes and permits at state park flood sites, refer to the Washington Parks website. Be sure to bring a hat, sunscreen, and plenty of water on your hikes.

Closest city or town: Odessa

How to get there: The Odessa Lake Creek Trail is one of many ways to access the Channeled Scablands. From Odessa, head west on W 1st Ave. toward S Alder St. and turn right at the first cross street onto WA-21 N/S Alder St. Continue to follow WA-21 N for 2.8 miles, then turn left onto Lakeview Ranch Loop N Dr. for 3.3 miles, turn right to stay on Lakeview Ranch Loop N, and in another 1.1 miles, the trailhead will be on your left.

GPS Coordinates: 47.4042° N, 118.7439° W

Did you know? The scablands were created 10,000-to-20,000 years ago by one of the biggest mega floods in world history.

Journal:

Date(s) Visited:

Weather
conditions:

Who you were with:

Nature observations:

Special memories:

Other Places

Place: _____

Date(s) visited:

Weather conditions:

Who you were with:

Nature observations:

Special memories:

Place: _____

Date(s) visited:

Weather conditions:

Who you were with:

Nature observations:

Special memories:

Place: _____

Date(s) visited:

Weather conditions:

Who you were with:

Nature observations:

Special memories:

Place: _____

Date(s) visited:

Weather conditions:

Who you were with:

Nature observations:

Special memories:

Place: _____

Date(s) visited:

Weather conditions:

Who you were with:

Nature observations:

Special memories:

Place: _____

Date(s) visited:

Weather conditions:

Who you were with:

Nature observations:

Special memories:

Place: _____

Date(s) visited:

Weather conditions:

Who you were with:

Nature observations:

Special memories:

Place: _____

Date(s) visited:

Weather conditions:

Who you were with:

Nature observations:

Special memories:

Place: _____

Date(s) visited:

Weather conditions:

Who you were with:

Nature observations:

Special memories:

Place: _____

Date(s) visited:

Weather conditions:

Who you were with:

Nature observations:

Special memories:

Credit the Incredible Photographers:

North Cascades

1) North Cascades National Park
https://search.creativecommons.org/photos/2eee0624-c4f4-466c-999c-e9abd37ff66c
"North Cascades National Park" by jeffgunn is licensed with CC BY 2.0. To view a copy of this license, visit https://creativecommons.org/licenses/by/2.0/

2) Mt. Baker-Snoqualmie National Forest
https://search.creativecommons.org/photos/2ac548ca-8b48-4af8-9a2d-9fd3d199ea18
"Mt. Baker-Snoqualmie National Forest" by jeffgunn is licensed with CC BY 2.0. To view a copy of this license, visit https://creativecommons.org/licenses/by/2.0/

3) Glacier Peak Wilderness
https://search.creativecommons.org/photos/2c90cd97-243f-49e3-83bb-18c4f3517865
"Glacier Peak Wilderness" by i8seattle is licensed with CC BY-NC 2.0. To view a copy of this license, visit https://creativecommons.org/licenses/by-nc/2.0/

4) Stehekin
https://search.creativecommons.org/photos/2068d858-cb26-47f8-b96a-cee935851d55
"Stehekin Landing" by Maurice King is licensed with CC BY 2.0. To view a copy of this license, visit https://creativecommons.org/licenses/by/2.0/

5) Horseshoe Basin
https://search.creativecommons.org/photos/ad28284e-0769-4d20-8ede-742897c20461
"Horseshoe Basin, Pasayten Wilderness, Okanogan Wenatchee National Forest" by Forest Service Pacific Northwest Region is marked under CC PDM 1.0. To view the terms, visit https://creativecommons.org/publicdomain/mark/1.0/

Central Cascades

6) Baring Mountain
https://search.creativecommons.org/photos/37132165-fe4b-4ecf-8caf-519da00e23e8
"Baring Mountain" by pfly is licensed with CC BY-SA 2.0. To view a copy of this license, visit https://creativecommons.org/licenses/by-sa/2.0/

7) Wallace Falls State Park
https://search.creativecommons.org/photos/dd8a87fe-102c-4fde-b3a4-91efcdb6d7d0
"Wallace Falls state park" by whatniccieate is licensed with CC BY 2.0. To view a copy of this license, visit https://creativecommons.org/licenses/by/2.0/

8) Okanogan-Wenatchee National Forest
https://search.creativecommons.org/photos/815956ed-b854-4a13-a53d-731a5a70ed47
"Sunrise at Wenatchee River, Okanogan Wenatchee National Forest" by Forest Service Pacific Northwest Region is marked under CC PDM 1.0. To view the terms, visit https://creativecommons.org/publicdomain/mark/1.0/

9) Alpine Lakes Wilderness
https://search.creativecommons.org/photos/eb3dd75d-a2e9-44d3-b43b-00a450a3e1da
"Alpine Lakes Wilderness, Okanogan-Wenatchee National Forest" by Forest Service Pacific Northwest Region is marked under CC PDM 1.0. To view the terms, visit https://creativecommons.org/publicdomain/mark/1.0/

10) Mount Sawyer
https://search.creativecommons.org/photos/82f29838-1268-427c-b2fa-e9a85a82b995
"Mt Sawyer 2015-09 - 21" by dierken is licensed with CC BY 2.0. To view a copy of this license, visit
https://creativecommons.org/licenses/by/2.0/

11) Granite Mountain https://search.creativecommons.org/photos/cf5c3768-edea-44ad-a69e-75bdeff4e628
"Granite Mountain Wilderness" by blmcalifornia is marked under CC PDM 1.0. To view the terms, visit
https://creativecommons.org/publicdomain/mark/1.0/

12) Olallie State Park
https://search.creativecommons.org/photos/a2155180-0db3-4abf-8bdb-8dcfea5e3afd
"We walked past the smart new entrance to Olallie State Park" by heystax is licensed with CC BY 2.0. To
view a copy of this license, visit https://creativecommons.org/licenses/by/2.0/

13) Rattlesnake Mountain Scenic Area
https://search.creativecommons.org/photos/05b39be0-dd33-44de-8536-f620dfece948
"rattlesnake mountain" by cluczkow is licensed with CC BY 2.0. To view a copy of this license, visit
https://creativecommons.org/licenses/by/2.0/

14) Kendall Katwalk
https://search.creativecommons.org/photos/eccd6941-e591-4f0d-a3c2-2ea965b2d925
"Kendall Katwalk" by kevin_oneill is licensed with CC BY-ND 2.0. To view a copy of this license, visit
https://creativecommons.org/licenses/by-nd/2.0/

15) Scenic Hot Springs
Scenic Hot Springs, Washington. (2020). Retrieved 2021, from https://scenichotsprings.blogspot.com/

-

Central Washington

16) Cleman Mountain https://search.creativecommons.org/photos/231f20be-c99e-426c-b3bc-06819619a713
"Cleman Mountain" by photomattick is licensed with CC BY-ND 2.0. To view a copy of this license, visit
https://creativecommons.org/licenses/by-nd/2.0/

17) Cowiche Canyon
https://search.creativecommons.org/photos/60157872-f2f4-455f-8cd2-56375349a53f
"Cowiche Canyon Recreation Site" by BLM Oregon & Washington is licensed with CC BY 2.0. To view a
copy of this license, visit https://creativecommons.org/licenses/by/2.0/

18) Sun Lakes-Dry Falls State Park
https://search.creativecommons.org/photos/c3d9520c-1864-4a17-a3a8-13826a5444b7
"Dry Falls" by gull@cyberspace.org is licensed with CC BY 2.0. To view a copy of this license, visit
https://creativecommons.org/licenses/by/2.0/

19) White Bluffs
https://search.creativecommons.org/photos/004c5326-5c24-48df-96e1-15a8a7b28c07
"White Bluffs, Hanford Reach National Monument" by HeatherHeatherHeather is licensed with CC BY 2.0.
To view a copy of this license, visit https://creativecommons.org/licenses/by/2.0/

20) Steamboat Rock State Park
https://search.creativecommons.org/photos/3c3cce0d-5798-4d2e-ba3e-8399de0e7eee
"2020--7 October--Steamboat Rock State Park hike" by LittleRoamingChief is licensed with CC BY 2.0. To
view a copy of this license, visit https://creativecommons.org/licenses/by/2.0/

21) Snake River
https://search.creativecommons.org/photos/39e2c221-7702-4461-884f-3bc7742ef267

"Snake River, Burbank, Washington" by Ken Lund is licensed with CC BY-SA 2.0. To view a copy of this license, visit https://creativecommons.org/licenses/by-sa/2.0/

Puget Sound and Islands

22) Lake Sammamish State Park
https://search.creativecommons.org/photos/172ff9d8-9042-45e6-85a7-e08214e3b16d
"Lake Sammamish State Park" by Marty the Adventurer is licensed with CC BY 2.0. To view a copy of this license, visit https://creativecommons.org/licenses/by/2.0/

23) Cattle Point Lighthouse
https://search.creativecommons.org/photos/56712f02-7517-497b-b6f7-7bcf52ca1622
"Cattle Point Lighthouse" by BLM Oregon & Washington is licensed with CC BY 2.0. To view a copy of this license, visit https://creativecommons.org/licenses/by/2.0/

24) Lopez Hill, Washington
Retrieved 2021, from
https://sanjuan.objects.liquidweb.services/photos/lopez_hill_lopez_island_photo_by_erin_wygant_4.jpg

-

25) Deception Pass State Park
https://search.creativecommons.org/photos/e11c0ae1-b683-4171-8bda-a936e63ae4c0
"Deception Pass State Park" by jeffgunn is licensed with CC BY 2.0. To view a copy of this license, visit https://creativecommons.org/licenses/by/2.0/

26) Padilla Bay
https://search.creativecommons.org/photos/3ae0b09a-e0fa-4571-8b10-30b068a67323
"Padilla Bay & San Juans" by lumachrome is licensed with CC BY-SA 2.0. To view a copy of this license, visit https://creativecommons.org/licenses/by-sa/2.0/

27) Larrabee State Park
https://search.creativecommons.org/photos/4dc13f2f-8f83-469e-8fe8-aa7f17ec59c6   "Larrabee State Park" by runarut is licensed with CC BY 2.0. To view a copy of this license, visit https://creativecommons.org/licenses/by/2.0/

28) Lime Kiln Point State Park
https://search.creativecommons.org/photos/aca7b9af-72f0-4bc5-963c-8dab400a1951
"File:Haro Strait at Lime Kiln Point.JPG" by Ian Poellet is licensed with CC BY-SA 3.0. To view a copy of this license, visit https://creativecommons.org/licenses/by-sa/3.0

Olympic Peninsula

29) Olympic National Park
https://search.creativecommons.org/photos/736cde09-bbd3-4d94-b1b6-e759e3b3f915
"wildflowers and lake, olympic national park" by ((brian)) is licensed with CC BY 2.0. To view a copy of this license, visit https://creativecommons.org/licenses/by/2.0/

30) Olympic National Forest
https://search.creativecommons.org/photos/c7795046-2a46-443c-9b34-2adbc3cbde5c
"Olympic mountain range, Olympic National Forest-2.jpg" by Forest Service Pacific Northwest Region is marked under CC PDM 1.0. To view the terms, visit https://creativecommons.org/publicdomain/mark/1.0/

31) Dungeness National Wildlife Refuge
https://search.creativecommons.org/photos/7874b29e-a38c-48cc-87ab-f91631201104
"File:Dungeness Spit sunset view.jpg" by Dicklyon is licensed with CC BY-SA 4.0. To view a copy of this license, visit https://creativecommons.org/licenses/by-sa/4.0

32) Rialto Beach
https://search.creativecommons.org/photos/e4a5143b-0d2f-40b5-bcf8-5d3c97042853
"Rialto Beach" by pfly is licensed with CC BY-SA 2.0. To view a copy of this license, visit
https://creativecommons.org/licenses/by-sa/2.0/

33) Cape Flattery
https://search.creativecommons.org/photos/eaa27daa-668f-4d29-9e8c-8ec91ed8e25f
"Cape Flattery" by Anupam_ts is licensed with CC BY-SA 2.0. To view a copy of this license, visit
https://creativecommons.org/licenses/by-sa/2.0/

34) La Push Beach
https://search.creativecommons.org/photos/e8ad7379-cfcd-43d5-9497-7955396e5e42
"La Push Beach, Washington, USA" by Lonni.besançon is licensed with CC BY-ND 2.0. To view a copy of
this license, visit https://creativecommons.org/licenses/by-nd/2.0/

Southwest Washington

35) Long Beach
https://search.creativecommons.org/photos/9327624b-1349-479c-8165-1cc1ca334304 "Welcome to Long
Beach, Washington" by jimmywayne is licensed with CC BY-NC-ND 2.0.
To view a copy of this license, visit https://creativecommons.org/licenses/by-nc-nd/2.0/

36) Cape Disappointment
https://search.creativecommons.org/photos/21143f8a-d875-4066-a0c4-60e9ae83b60e
"Cape Disappointment" by spi516 is licensed with CC BY-SA 2.0. To view a copy of this license, visit
https://creativecommons.org/licenses/by-sa/2.0/

37) Columbia River Gorge National Scenic Area
https://search.creativecommons.org/photos/0e8a3268-a993-4755-bbf0-f53b4135702f
"Mosier Twin Tunnel Trail in Fall-Columbia River Gorge" by Forest Service Pacific Northwest Region is
marked under CC PDM 1.0. To view the terms, visit https://creativecommons.org/publicdomain/mark/1.0/

South Cascades

38) Mount Rainier
https://search.creativecommons.org/photos/8fd586ec-acb6-49b3-9c7c-ed936430d6c0
"Mount Rainier" by tiffany98101 is licensed with CC BY 2.0. To view a copy of this license, visit
https://creativecommons.org/licenses/by/2.0/

39) Nisqually River
https://search.creativecommons.org/photos/7513ec6e-efad-458a-8a9b-5e4a11311a5b
"Nisqually River" by Mount Rainier NPS is licensed with CC BY 2.0. To view a copy of this license, visit
https://creativecommons.org/licenses/by/2.0/

40) Gifford Pinchot National Forest
https://search.creativecommons.org/photos/68aea9aa-19b9-4d36-8e83-71c85e0ccfde
"596 Gifford Pinchot National Forest, pre-eruptive Mt St Helens" by Forest Service Pacific Northwest
Region is marked under CC PDM 1.0. To view the terms, visit
https://creativecommons.org/publicdomain/mark/1.0/

41) Indian Heaven
https://search.creativecommons.org/photos/785460d9-00f9-4ab7-a372-a87dfbc0e589
"Camping Indian Heaven" by sprague is licensed with CC BY 2.0. To view a copy of this license, visit
https://creativecommons.org/licenses/by/2.0/

42) Goat Rocks Wilderness

125

Eastern Washington

43) Lewis and Clark Trail State Park

44) Blue Mountains

45) Palouse Falls

46) Columbia Plateau Trail State Park

47) Colville National Forest

48) Selkirk Range

49) Riverside State Park

50) Channeled Scablands

Washington Map